The OBAMA FAMILY Photo Album

Celebrating
PRESIDENT
BARACK OBAMA
in Pictures

Jane Katirgis

Enslow Publishers, Inc.
40 Industrial Road
Box 398
Berkeley Heights, NJ 07922
USA
http://www.enslow.com

For our nephews and nieces—
Andreas, Penny, Jimmy, Michael, Brendan, Joseph, Matthew,
Mary Cate, Penny, Bryan, Costa, and Brigid—
one of whom may be president someday.

Library of Congress Cataloging-in-Publication Data:
Katirgis, Jane.
 Celebrating President Barack Obama in pictures / Jane Katirgis.
     p. cm. — (The Obama family photo album)
 Includes bibliographical references and index.
 Summary: "Photographs illustrate the life of President Barack Obama from childhood with a focus on his role as President of the United States"—Provided by publisher.
 ISBN-13: 978-0-7660-3651-2
 ISBN-10: 0-7660-3651-0
 1. Obama, Barack—Pictorial works—Juvenile literature. 2. Presidents—United States—Biography—Pictorial works—Juvenile literature. I. Title.
 E908.K37 2009
 973.932092—dc22
 [B]

2009010558

Printed in the United States of America

10 9 8 7 6 5 4 3 2 1

To Our Readers:
We have done our best to make sure all Internet Addresses in this book were active and appropriate when we went to press. However, the author and the publisher have no control over and assume no liability for the material available on those Internet sites or on other Web sites they may link to. Any comments or suggestions can be sent by e-mail to comments@enslow.com or to the address on the back cover.

♻ Enslow Publishers, Inc., is committed to printing our books on recycled paper. The paper in every book contains 10% to 30% post-consumer waste (PCW). The cover board on the outside of each book contains 100% PCW. Our goal is to do our part to help young people and the environment too!

Photo Credits: Allen Fredrickson/Reuters/Landov, p. 15; Associated Press, pp. 1, 6 (top), 7, 8, 9 (top and bottom), 10, 11, 12, 13, 17, 20, 22, 23, 25, 27, 28, 29, 30; Brian Snyder/Reuters/Landov, p. 14; Department of Defense, p. 21 (top); Reuters/Larry Downing/Landov, p. 21 (bottom); John Gress/Reuters/Landov, p. 16; Kevin Dietsch/Bloomberg News/Landov, p. 3; Kevin Lamarque/Reuters/Landov, pp. 18–19, 31; Larry Downing/Reuters/Landov, p. 26; Reuters/Landov, p. 6 (bottom); White House Photo by Pete Souza, p. 24; Zhang Yah/Xinhua/Landov, p. 5.

Cover Photo: Ron Sachs/UPI/Landov

Contents

A Historic President

On November 4, 2008, people across the United States and around the world waited for the election results. Barack Obama and John McCain had both been campaigning for over a year, each hoping to become the next president. After the votes were counted, Barack Obama was declared the winner. When he walked onstage with his wife, Michelle, and their two daughters, the crowd went wild.

Many people looked forward to the change Obama promised to bring to the U.S. government. But they were also excited for another reason: Barack Obama had made history. He was the first African American to be elected United States president.

Growing Up

Barack Hussein Obama was born on August 4, 1961, in Honolulu, Hawaii. His mother, Ann Dunham, was from Kansas. His father, Barack Obama, Sr., was from Kenya. They were divorced in 1964, and his father moved back to Africa. Barack stayed in Hawaii with his mother.

Barack Obama, age nine, sits with his mother; his stepfather, Lolo Soetoro; and his baby sister, Maya Soetoro. The family had moved to Indonesia when Barack was six years old.

When Barack was ten, he moved back to Hawaii and lived with his grandparents, Stanley and Madelyn Dunham. He called his grandmother "Toot," short for *Tutu*, the Hawaiian word for grandmother.

*T*his photo was taken during the only visit Barack, age ten,
ever had with his father after the divorce. His father died
in a car accident in 1982.

College and Career

*B*arack Obama is shown here as a college student in New York City. After graduating from high school, he attended Occidental College in Los Angeles for two years. Then he decided to go to Columbia University in New York City. He received his college degree in political science in 1983.

*A*fter he graduated from Harvard Law School in 1991, Obama worked in Chicago to help people register to vote.

*O*bama was a professor at the University of Chicago Law School from 1992 to 2004. ▶

Husband and Father

arack Obama and Michelle Robinson met at a law firm in Chicago. They were married on October 18, 1992, in Chicago.

Barack and Michelle have two daughters. Malia was born in 1998, and Sasha was born in 2001. Here, Barack walks on the beach with Malia, left, and Sasha during a vacation in Hawaii.

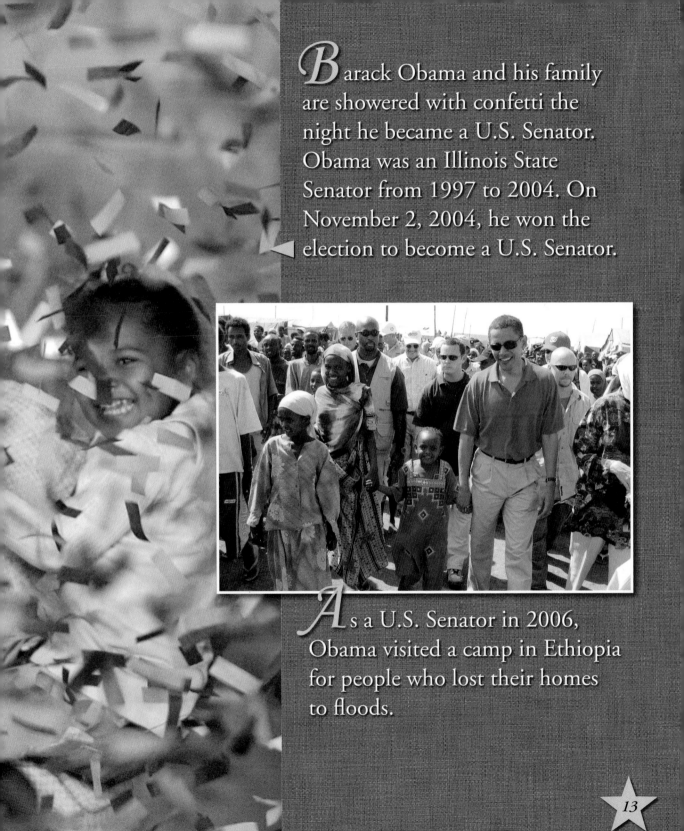

Barack Obama and his family are showered with confetti the night he became a U.S. Senator. Obama was an Illinois State Senator from 1997 to 2004. On November 2, 2004, he won the election to become a U.S. Senator.

As a U.S. Senator in 2006, Obama visited a camp in Ethiopia for people who lost their homes to floods.

Campaign for President

*O*n February 10, 2007, Barack Obama announced that he would run for president. He traveled across the country, speaking to crowds.

*S*enator Barack Obama shakes hands with students and supporters at a campaign rally at Dartmouth College in Hanover, New Hampshire.

15

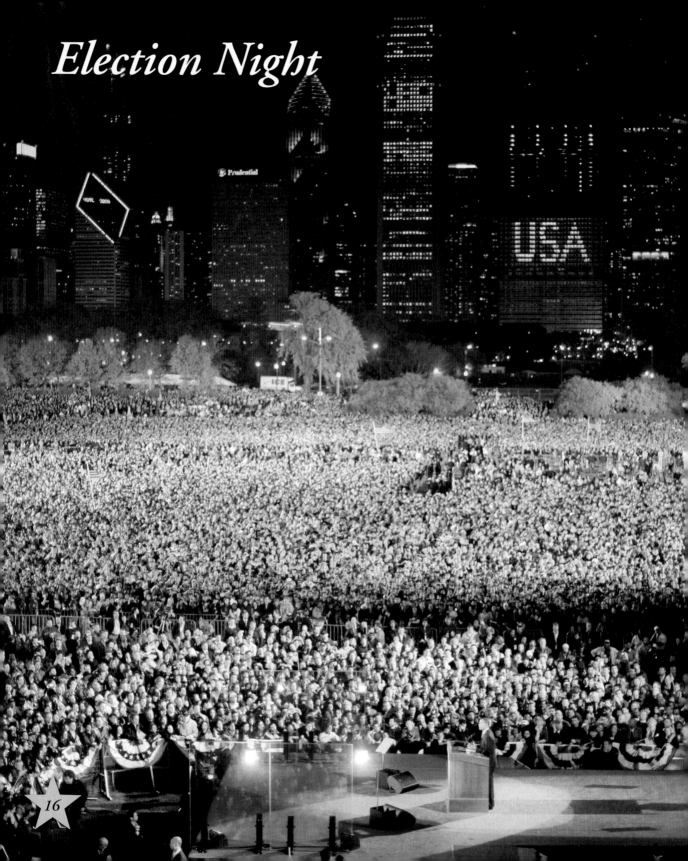

Election Night

*B*arack Obama was declared the winner of the 2008 presidential election. Barack, Sasha, Malia, and Michelle Obama wave to the crowd of about 240,000 people at the election night rally in Chicago, Illinois, on November 4, 2008.

*D*uring his victory speech, Obama said, "If there is anyone out there who still doubts that America is a place where all things are possible, who still wonders if the dream of our founders is alive in our time, who still questions the power of our democracy, tonight is your answer."

President-Elect

*Former President
George H.W.
Bush*

*President-elect
Barack Obama*

*President
George W. Bush*

Ｐresident George W. Bush invited
President-elect Barack Obama to the
White House, along with all the living
former presidents.

*Former President
Bill Clinton*

*Former President
Jimmy Carter*

19

Some Time for Fun

*P*resident-elect Barack
Obama body surfs in
Honolulu, Hawaii,
during Christmas
vacation in 2008.

*O*bama rebounds the ball during a basketball game with U.S. military service members.

*T*he president enjoys taking a walk with the family's dog, Bo, on the South Lawn of the White House.

Inauguration Day

*B*arack Obama was sworn in as the 44th President of the United States on January 20, 2009. He gives his inaugural address at the U.S. Capitol building in Washington, D.C.

*W*hile Michelle Obama holds the same Bible that Abraham Lincoln used at his inauguration, Barack Obama takes the oath of office. Malia and Sasha look on proudly.

President at Work

*B*arack Obama speaks to military personnel during a visit to Camp Victory in Baghdad, Iraq, on April 7, 2009. This was the last stop of his first trip to Europe as president. ▶

*P*resident Obama talks on the phone in the Oval Office of the White House.

Community Life in D.C.

*P*resident Barack Obama is joined by his family as he reads "Where the Wild Things Are" at the 2009 Easter Egg Roll on the South Lawn of the White House on April 13, 2009. Over 30,000 people came to the event for a day of fun and games.

*O*bama visits the Sasha Bruce House, a shelter for teens, in Washington, D.C. He helped paint one of the rooms at the home as part of the National Day of Service Project.

Meeting with World Leaders

*P*art of the president's job is to meet with leaders from other countries. Here, President Obama visits with Japan's Prime Minister Taro Aso. They are talking in the Oval Office of the White House.

*P*resident Barack Obama and Canadian Prime Minister Stephen Harper walk down the Hall of Honor for a news conference in Canada.

Getting Around in the Air

When the president needs to fly somewhere, he first takes a helicopter called Marine One. The helicopter takes him to the Air Force One airplane.

President Obama boards Air Force One. He is ready for another day as president.

Further Reading

Books

Gorman, Jacqueline Laks. *Who Leads Our Country?* Pleasantville, N.Y.: Weekly Reader Books, 2008.

Grimes, Nikki. *Barack Obama: Son of Promise, Child of Hope.* New York: Simon & Schuster Books for Young Readers, 2008.

The National Children's Book and Literacy Alliance. *Our White House: Looking In, Looking Out.* Somerville, Mass.: Candlewick Press, 2008.

Internet Addresses

Kids.gov. *The Official Kids' Portal for the U.S. Government.* http://www.kids.gov

PBS Kids. "President For a Day." http://pbskids.org/democracy/presforaday/

Index